2-19-94

Bill & Pat

We enjoyed our time with
you. We are thankful for
you. We are thankful for
the snow and we are
for your friendship!

Bob & Marie

CRESTED BUTTE
THE EDGE OF PARADISE

CRESTED BUTTE
THE EDGE OF PARADISE

Photography by Nathan Bilow
Text by Sandy Fails

Published by Jeffery Neumann, Crested Butte Publishing, Crested Butte, Colorado

Opening page photo: Horses graze on green fields south of Crested Butte, but skiers can still find plenty of spring snow on the slopes of Paradise Divide northwest of town.

Title page photo: Streetlights and early-morning fog create haloes along Elk Avenue and lend the Old Town Hall a ghostly glow.

Previous page photo: Reed Meredith blasts through fresh powder on the North Face. In an hour, he'll be back at work as the director of the resort's children's center, but chances are he is *not* thinking about work at this moment.

Published and distributed by Crested Butte Printing, P.O. Box 1030, Crested Butte, Colorado 81224 (303) 349-7511

ISBN 0-9624198-1-8
First Printing 1989; second printing 1990; third printing 1992

Printed by Crested Butte Printing, Box 1030, Crested Butte, Colorado 81224
Bound by Mountain States Bindery, Salt Lake City, Utah
Color Separations by Orent Graphics, Omaha, Nebraska
Design by Sandy Fails, with counsel from Michael Garren and Tony Fortunato..

CONTENTS

PREFACE

Crested Butte, to quote former silver miner John Hahn, "just gets a hold on you." Maybe it's the enveloping mountains, at once awesome and inviting. Or the Victorian mining town, unbroken link to a romanticized past. Maybe it's the people, open and friendly, or the recreational bounty. Or perhaps it's all of these, plus some intangible quality to this place and its people, a sense of caring, heartiness and irreverence, a connection to the Earth and each other.

Whatever the pull, loyalties to Crested Butte form quickly and grow deeply, in people who have lived here eighty years or three; second-home owners and first-time visitors.

Photographer Nathan Bilow, printer Jeff Neumann, and I have also fallen under Crested Butte's spell. In this book, we'd like to continue the statement so many people start: "There's something about this place..."

Tony Mihelich pauses at the window of the store he's run for decades, the Conoco station and Crested Butte Hardware store. Tony, with his quiet, kind face, reminds passersby that Crested Butte isn't just another resort town.

7

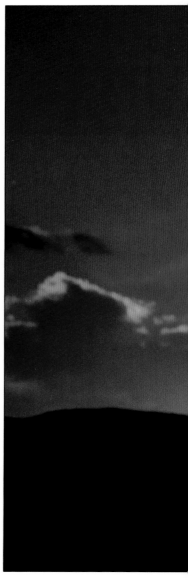

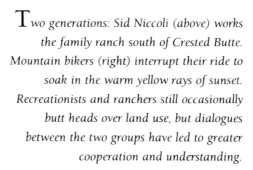

*Two generations: Sid Niccoli (above) works
the family ranch south of Crested Butte.
Mountain bikers (right) interrupt their ride to
soak in the warm yellow rays of sunset.
Recreationists and ranchers still occasionally
butt heads over land use, but dialogues
between the two groups have led to greater
cooperation and understanding.*

As I write, the tilted computer screen shows just how decisively the
floor of this old miner's house lists to the east. The roof leaks, the doors
stick, and the windows whistle in the slightest breeze. But the crackling
fire gives a glow to wooden walls; the house feels cozy and welcoming;
and my family affectionately calls it home.

Ah, but it's not just ours. For all our years of patching and hammering,
painting and curtain hanging, this house holds on to some life of its own.
For 100 years before we rolled into town full of youthful energy, this
house sheltered some of the people who shaped Crested Butte. And the

love and drama of their lives holds tenaciously to the walls like some kind of benevolent ghost.

I sense the same thing about the town of Crested Butte. For eight years, I've voted in her elections, helped with her celebrations, written editorials to shape her future. This is my home, my family's home. But when I hear Willard and Ronnie Ruggera swapping stories of Crested Butte's olden days, I remember just how much deeper other roots sink into this mountain soil.

Those old stories — of roof-high snows, mining disasters, town-wide sledding parties — reveal the labor, perseverence and sense of humor required to forge a home in such harsh environs. But the telling of the stories and the interactions of the storytellers show an underlying gentleness of spirit that seems an equally important part of Crested Butte's legacy. The town's younger residents may have life a little easier these days with snowplows and chair lifts, and their energy may occasionally have a reckless edge to it, but the traditions of working hard, playing hard, and caring for each other remain intact.

Now it's mainly the younger folks who paint the buildings and fill the council chambers. We clap ourselves on the back for the latest marketing coups, school campaigns, or fundraisers. We give a lot to this town, and the town gives back. But that old intangible feeling that holds Crested Butte's residents and visitors to this place seems to lead directly back to the town's original residents.

Crested Butte has cleared my head, toughened my skin and touched my heart. I've been infatuated with her, fed up with her, cramped and charmed by her. I've made the mud season escape to catch some big-city bright lights. And I've always returned to the mountains with that deep, welcome sense of coming home.

This book is an expression of our love for Crested Butte and our thanks. Thanks to the people whose concern and energy today carry Crested Butte through challenging times. Thanks to the guests who feed the economy and help preserve the town. And, most of all, thanks to Crested Butte's elders, the people who molded the town and now generously share their home and hearts with us.

Sandy Fails

Visiting skiers often stop in amazement as small bodies fly by. Local kids sometimes learn to ski soon after learning to walk and by adolescence are racers and hot doggers. Not a bad place to grow up.

10

E_{ach} season brings moments of
beauty and stillness. Moonrise over a
snowy slope (above) creates a simple
pastel landscape; a field of fireweed
paints a livelier image.

CRESTED BUTTE

THE EDGE OF PARADISE

Imagine the most spectacular mountain wilderness in Colorado. In a small valley in its midst, put a charming town where unpainted miner's shacks lurch drunkenly toward trim Victorian doll houses. Populate the town with oldtimers still polkaing and pot-lucking; young people powered by endorphins and convictions; families sending down roots; and city-dwelling fans who escape to the mountains every chance they get.

Then, three miles up a winding road, put a modern ski resort, with some of the state's boldest ski terrain and lodging for 6,000 guests in condominiums, lodges and a luxury hotel. Next, place a renowned golf course and country club just down the road.

Throw in a few hundred inches of winter snow and the grandest summer wildflower display in the universe.

Welcome to Crested Butte, Colorado.

Early-morning fog silhouettes a sleeping downtown Crested Butte, with Crested Butte Mountain in the background. Previous page: Antique streetlights enhance Elk Avenue's classic profile.

Cradled by four wilderness areas in south central Colorado (the Raggeds, Maroon Bells, West Elks and Collegiate Peaks), Crested Butte lies at the end of the road, the jumping-off point between civilization and backcountry. The mountains rise suddenly and the world slows down as you near the town limits. Traffic (meaning a few cars, horse-drawn carriages, fat tire bikes, sleds...) creeps to 15 m.p.h.

Bench-sitting, a lost art in the modern world, endures on Elk Avenue, especially in the sun-warmed days of spring and summer. With the mountains a constant backdrop, Tony Verzuh and Pitsker Sporcich, mountain buddhas in worn brown sweaters, warm the bench outside Tony's Conoco, making room and small talk for occasional younger guests. In contrast to their quiet vigil, the Company Store bench hops as the social headquarters for various frisky canines and humans, tanning their torsos and honing their hacky-sack skills. The school kids seldom sit, but caroom bikes and skateboards over homemade ramps or drag their sleds to the local sledding hill.

Beyond the bench-side festivities, a glance down Elk Avenue frames a century of quiet perseverence. Shadows fall on false-fronted buildings where miners and fortune-seekers bought supplies a century ago. No museum of dead relics, this town has continued to live despite the odds

Crested Butte as viewed from the air (right) appears as an isolated pocket of civilization in a wilderness of mountains.

*S*now still claims the Paradise
Divide peaks northwest of Crested
Butte in this May photograph, but
spring marches steadily up the valley.

against it. Natural disasters, economic collapses, epidemics and almost continuous hardship — still not enough to squelch the character and determination of the people, who just wove their friendships more tightly, sent their roots ever deeper, and soaked more inspiration from the surrounding ethereal beauty.

From a distance, downtown Crested Butte appears picturebook quaint; at closer range, the sagging boards and splintery window sills recall countless harsh winters. George Sibley, former *Crested Butte Chronicle* editor, described them in his book, **Part of a Winter**: "They didn't look like buildings in danger of falling down, but like buildings trying to get comfortable."

A few buildings remain almost unchanged from the faded photos of decades ago: Tony's Conoco, the Old Rock School, Stefanic's Grocery, the jail. But most have donned bright colors and modern uses; the Old

20

Croatian Hall, once host to community polkas, now serves guests and locals as the elegant Crested Butte Club, with athletic club facilities, Victorian guests suites and pub.

While downtown Crested Butte's bright colors and lycra-clad residents might startle the miners of 90 years ago, the scene up Gothic Road would flabbergast them. Just three miles north, Mt. Crested Butte offers a modern world of condominiums, luxury hotel and conference center, shopping malls, restaurants and new homes perched on slopes that roll up toward the summit of Crested Butte Mountain.

One of the top ten ski areas in Colorado, Crested Butte Mountain Resort tallies more than 400,000 skier days each winter. Once a mom-and-pop ski area where the president also cleaned the bathrooms, CBMR has fought its way toward the top in a fiercely competitive industry. The technology has grown more expensive, the market tighter, and the stakes higher.

Skyland's renowned golf course and country club has helped entice new fans to Crested Butte; guests now come in private planes as well as patched-up Volkswagen vans. While an occasional "Gone Fishin'" sign shows up on a store door during mud season, the restaurants and shops have become more professional and diverse to serve the new clientele. Personal service no longer means the chef knows who wants magic mushrooms sneaked into their smoothies.

In Mt. Crested Butte's town council chambers, heretofore foreign

Despite differences in jobs, ages, and lifestyles, Crested Butte's people share a commitment to the town and its quality of life. Jeff Vicker (far left) discusses his traditional pottery techniques (using underground firing and local clay) with customers at the Festival of the Arts. County and Municipal Judge Jerry Reese (center) looks very official in his black robe; by evening he'll be back at his Cement Creek Ranch in jeans and hiking boots. Rudy Verzuh and Tony Orazem (right) visit at the Two Buttes Senior Center.

words like "traffic" and "crowds" sneak into planning sessions. And CBMR execs bring to the board room increasingly crafty strategies to turn Crested Butte's beauty, charm, and recreational bounty into hot commodities.

But while growing ever more sophisticated as a resort, Crested Butte remains doggedly unsophisticated in its private life. People here take life a little differently. For some, security means having six cords of wood

*J*im *Talbot, Allison Finch and Tuck round up the horses for Fantasy Ranch. Fantasy Ranch offers hourly, daily, overnight and custom horseback rides, with lively horses far from typical dude ranch fare.*

chopped and stacked and an elk in the freezer by October. Career advancement means being promoted from busperson to waitperson at Donita's. Punctual means, well, sort of. Material wealth means having a $1200 high-tech mountain bike, $1500 state-of-the-art kayak and twelve pairs of skis beside your shack of a house and crippled $400 Volkswagen van.

For the growing number of families and professionals, life may

DOUBLES
ONLY

DOUBLES
ONLY

TRIPLES
ONLY

TRIPLES
ONLY

The extremes of the sport: Spring break brings rare crowds
to the Keystone chair lift (above); during the same week, two
backcountry skiers (right) invest a little effort to find huge
expanses of untracked powder.

Fun comes in all forms in Crested Butte. Former President Jimmy Carter (above) plays Karnac the Magnificent during a comedy night fundraiser for Crested Butte's Physically Challenged Ski Program. His wife, Rosalyn Carter, serves as a board member for the program. The fun gets a little splashier for Deven Bennett as he attempts to catch a water balloon (far right) during Fourth of July festivities on Elk Avenue, and for Mitch Hoffman (right), stopping to squeeze the water out of his socks after a mountain bike river crossing.

incorporate retirement plans, lawn mowers and orthodontist bills, but crime and status symbols haven't made it to Crested Butte yet. The marshal, the mayor and a local dishwasher play on the same softball team, and nobody brings his title with him to the softball field.

The preferred form of celebration remains the potluck, varying from formal potlucks for weddings to casual potlucks springing spontaneously from warm summer afternoons.

Greed, distrust and apathy, almost required for urban survival, wither in the high-altitude sunshine. Caring and openness, political activism, and community involvement thrive. If that sometimes brings uncomfortable scrutiny to local businesses, individuals or governments, it also brings much-needed support when times grow harsh.

This is life on the edge of paradise. In winter, work starts when you dig out the snowed-in walkway in sub-zero morning darkness and ends only when the woodstove crackles with a new fire in the evening. In between, you work your jobs, as many as you can juggle, to tide you over during the laid-back, penny-pinching spring and autumn. Paychecks are as thin as the air, cultural opportunities as rare as fast food. But beauty shines in the mountains, the wildflowers, and the faces of people who love their home and their neighbors.

An enduring small-town charm defies the cynicism escalating all around. And no matter how many revelers share the streets and slopes by day, the evenings bring starshine, perhaps a hint of pinon on the air, and silence enough to hear your own thoughts.

The brilliant hues of summer. Gail
Burford and Renee Balevre (right)
pedal their mountain bikes along a
path lined with wildflowers. During
Aerial Weekend (above), hot air
balloons spread the color to the
morning sky. Almost two dozen hot
air balloons take off from Mt.
Crested Butte's base area, while
spectators feast their eyes and snap
their camera shutters.

THE MOUNTAINS

NATURE'S ARTISTRY

Dwarfing Crested Butte's small, century-old outpost of civilization, the surrounding mountains showcase almost two billion years of nature's artistry. Volcanoes and glaciers, steady erosion and violent shifts in the Earth's surface sculpted dramatic peaks and valleys, now painted by the snows of winter, wildflowers of summer and golden aspens of autumn. Hundreds of species of plants and animals revel in the lush summers and use a little evolutionary magic to survive the intense winters. In no place does nature more generously share her repertoire than in Crested Butte's backyard.

Fireweed and daisies flash their colors against a cloud-dotted sky. Just another perfect day in paradise. Previous page: Aspens gleam yellow-gold against the crags of Mt. Crested Butte on this September day.

*C*apitol Peak, a 14,000-foot
mountain north of Crested Butte,
catches the last rays of sunlight,
giving its summit an eerie orange
glow against the darkening sky.

Visitors are struck first by this area's beauty, then by its diversity. Every point on the compass offers a unique view, panoramic or microscopic — the red strata of Teocalli, the rugged rock dikes towering above Lake Irwin, the white granite pinnacles of Gothic and Crested Butte mountains, each with its own plant and animal populations. Just north of Crested Butte, six peaks tower above 14,000 feet (Castle, Pyramid, North and South Maroon, Snowmass and Capitol); just south of town, cattle and horses graze on open ranchlands.

The variety comes partly from the vastness of nature's canvas. Four wilderness areas surrounding Crested Butte — the Raggeds, West Elks, Maroon Bells and Collegiate Peaks — and extensive national forests preserve several hundred thousand acres of land relatively unmarred by humans. More than eighty percent of Gunnison County's land is controlled by federal or state agencies. And in a county larger than Delaware and twice the size of Rhode Island, the population stands at approximately 10,000 people. Standing on most peaks around Crested Butte, climbers see no sign of human activity except the scars of old mining roads.

Yet even for its vast size, the wilderness around Crested Butte shows unusual diversity in both geology and biology. Western State College (WSC) geology professor Bruce Bartleson called the area "one of the more unusual places in the United States in the variety of ages and rock

Bluebells shimmer against dark green foliage. At their peak, bluebells cover whole hillsides with tiny blue spots of iridescence.

Rich shades of green color the earth during summer's brief reign. Above, sunshine behind false helibore (called skunk cabbage locally) creates a luminous pattern. Slopes curving into the East River Valley (right) mix lush green with the deep red of sedimentary rock. The sedimentary layers were formed by the erosion of an ancient mountain range, the Ancestral Rockies.

*F*erns and wildflowers form a
natural work of art. Two months
before, snow covered this ground; in
two months, snow will cover it again.
But for now, the surrounding forest
looks as tropical and lush as its
equatorial cousins.

types." Rocks near here represent every major era of geologic history — Precambrian, Paleozoic, Mesozoic, and Cenozoic. WSC geologist Thomas Prather wrote in his book, **Geology of the Gunnison Country,** "Examples of most types of geologic phenomena are represented — such as vulcanism, intrusive igneous activity, hot springs, metamorphism, folding and faulting, glaciation, and fossils of ancient creatures ranging from brachiopods to dinosaurs. The area even has examples of beaches, limestone banks and deserts from the distant geologic past."

Some of the Elk Mountains' most dramatic formations were caused by igneous intrusive activity, where molten rock — magma — moving below the surface pushed into weaker overlaying rock. Magma flowing into cracks in sedimentary rocks created the dikes near Lake Irwin; the dikes were exposed as the softer surrounding rock eroded away. Crested Butte, Marcellina and Gothic mountains, with their grandiose arches, formed when molten rock shoved its way upward beneath weak layers of shale, then cooled and hardened before reaching the surface. The gothic-looking pinnacles of these mountains were later exposed by erosion of the shale covering them. Much larger magma bodies pushed upward and formed huge mounds called stocks, sometimes several mountains' worth, such as the white granite Snowmass Stock that comprises Snowmass and Capitol mountains.

Winter's tranquil beauty. Ski tracks (far left) decorate the new-fallen snow on the Ruby Range slopes just behind the Irwin Lodge. The lodge ten miles west of Crested Butte offers snowcat and helicopter skiing on slopes like these. Above, sunshine breaks through passing storm clouds, highlighting snow-covered branches; and a ptarmigan, with its feathery snowshoes, stands motionless and almost invisible in the field of white.

Intense heat from the magma sometimes caused contact metamorphism, radically altering the adjoining rock. For example, contact metamorphism turned dark gray Leadville Limestone into the snow white marble that gave the town of Marble northwest of Crested Butte its economy and its name.

Volcanic activity shaped much of the West Elk range south and west of Crested Butte. A huge volcano that once overlooked the current site of Gunnison created volcanic debris — breccia — that was carried by mudslides and melting snows to create formations like the Dillon Pinnacles near Blue Mesa Reservoir and the Castles.

Ever curious, marmots (sometimes called whistlepigs) often waddle out to their rock rooftops to stare at passing humans. Don't laugh at this marmot's pot belly; stored fat will keep him alive during his nine-month winter nap. While marmots hibernate, larger animals such as elk (far right) migrate to lower elevations to survive the winter.

In contrast to the more violent volcanic activity, sedimentary rocks laid down over millions of years make up several mountains north of Crested Butte, such as the Maroon Bells, Avery Peak and Teocalli Mountain. The erosion of a former mountain range, the Ancestral Rockies, formed stratifications that were later uplifted and eroded to create these Modern Rockies. In some areas, such as near Schofield Park and south toward Crested Butte, the sedimentary rocks were then folded and twisted for spectacular effect. The rocks around Schofield and in places along West Maroon Pass have actually been turned upside down.

Glaciers, which melted a scant 10,000 years ago, also did their part to carve out valleys and cirques in the mountains. Whetstone Mountain, originally formed by igneous intrusion, was then scrubbed to its current shape by glaciers. The Slate River and East River valleys are classic glacial valleys.

The varied landscape and altitude around Crested Butte translates

Shorter days and cooler temperatures prompt a parade of gold and rust in September. Aspens steal the show with their shimmery gold leaves, shown here along West Brush Creek Road (left), just peeking through on the northwest side of Mt. Emmons (center), and striping the view of the rock dikes of the Ruby Range near Lake Irwin (right).

into varied plant and animal life as well. More than seven decades ago, WSC biology professor Dr. John C. Johnson stumbled on the Gothic area eight miles north of Crested Butte and later described it as "a region rich in both fauna and flora, far above anything I'd seen elsewhere in Colorado...Not only was the plant and animal life there exceedingly abundant but it proved to be extremely rich in the number of different species, due largely to the abundant moisture and the great variation in altitude."

For $200, Dr. Johnson bought the old seventy-acre ghost town of Gothic with its twenty-two buildings and started the Rocky Mountain Biological Laboratory. Now one of the oldest and most respected high-altitude biological field stations in the world, RMBL draws biologists and students from universities around the country to study subjects ranging from acid rain to social heirarchies among marmots.

Researchers at RMBL have identified more than 600 species of wildflowers in the Gothic area; more than 300 of those survive on the barren-looking slopes above treeline. Crested Butte's showiest flowers —hot pink fireweed, scarlet gilia, lupine, columbine, sunflowers — impress the laziest roadside explorers. But a little hiking and eye-balling reveals the earth-hugging flowers of the high alpine regions, called "belly plants" by biologist Paul Buck, who has spent many an hour on his belly studying them.

As though eager to enjoy Crested Butte's summers, some wildflowers, like glacier lilies and marsh marigolds, poke through the melting snow as early as May. But the wildflower show around Crested Butte generally peaks in mid to late July, with profuse splashes of color covering the hillsides. The parade of color gradually marches up the landscape; as various species are fading at lower altitudes, they may be just poking through the ground at high elevations. But plants that at 8,000 feet elevation reach a height of several feet may grow only a few inches tall at 11,000 feet elevation. Gnarled and twisted fur trees several hundred years old battle the cold, bitter winds and short growing seasons just below treeline (approximately 11,500 feet elevation) to grow a few feet tall.

Wildflower species differ greatly with altitude and terrain, but variety may also exist in a small area. In many meadows, a dozen or more different species bloom within a few square feet, to the delight of

W*ildflowers of all shapes and
colors grace the hillsides around
Crested Butte: Bowed sunflowers (far
left), asters and paintbrush (above),
and fireweed (left).*

Everyday details of the summer landscape turn into objets d'art in the late afternoon sunshine: Hanging aspen leaves and a single daisy blossom backlit by the sun (left) and a glacier lily field brilliant with yellow and green.

A bald eagle flies against the evening sky — a rare and special sight. Bald eagles are most often sighted by observant passersby south of Crested Butte near Almont.

photographers, wildflower buffs, bumblebees and biologists. Crested Butte's wildflower cornucopia in 1988 even received official recognition in the political sector when Governor Roy Romer proclaimed Crested Butte the state's official wildflower capital.

In addition to their abundance and variety of wildflowers, the Elk Mountains host some rare plants as well. RMBL biologists have found several endemic species — found only on certain local mountaintops — probably abandoned there when the glaciers retreated 10,000 years ago. One type of sunflower found only on high ridges is probably rare because it is new and has not had time to expand its range. A species of flightless grasshopper also lives in these mountains; perhaps the adaptation keeps the grasshopper from being borne by alpine winds to nearby hostile environments.

Like Crested Butte's human occupants, the plants and animals in the mountains work a little harder than their flatland cousins. Many plants and insects have evolved a kind of natural antifreeze; trees may also shed moisture as cool weather approaches to avoid the freezing and bursting of their cells. Most plants in this environment are perennial, storing large quantities of energy below-ground during the winter. This allows them to grow, flower and set seed in approximately a hundred days.

A few animals also seek shelter underground, sleeping up to nine

Glimpses of the valley's wild occupants: A squirrel feasts on summer's abundant flora and a big-eared fawn relies on his camouflage coloring for safety from predators.

Mountainscapes: *The peak of Whetstone Mountain, still snowy, reflects in a hidden lake in mid-summer (left); Jim Talbot leads horseback riders past dramatic rock formations along West Maroon Pass (right); and light and shadow play along the northern slopes of the glacier-formed East River Valley.*

months a year while winter reigns. Young marmots, beaver-like mammals born and reared underground until emerging in June, have three months to triple their body weight for their first hibernation; half don't make it through the winter. The only other true hibernators here are the Golden Mantled Ground Squirrel and the Jumping Mouse. In true hibernation, an animal's respiration and heart rate slow drastically (perhaps one breath every couple of minutes) and its body temperature lowers to that of its environment. A few animals, like bears, go into a torpor state, sleeping deeply and living off their own stored body fat.

The mammals who stay active during the winter — such as coyotes, foxes, snowshoe hares, voles, field mice, pocket gophers, martens and weasels — adapt their diets, habits, sometimes even their appearance for the winter. Hares, weasels, and ptarmigans change to white to disguise themselves against the snow. White fur also insulates better; no melanin allows for dead air spaces. Ptarmigans also grow feathers around their feet in the winter, creating a kind of natural snowshoe, and can tunnel beneath the snow for greater protection. Larger animals like elk and deer migrate to lower elevations for the winter.

Sensing greater danger in the winter, most wild animals become much more shy when the snows come. But in summer's early mornings or late afternoons, patient humans can sometimes view their wild neighbors, particularly at the edges of meadows or scree fields. The area's squirrels and other rodents, hummingbirds, robins, magpies, deer and ever-curious marmots are most commonly seen; bears, porcupines, elk, bighorn sheep, skunks, bats, coyotes, foxes, badgers, beavers, weasels, golden eagles, boreal owls and falcons are less visible occupants.

While humans here have carved out a seemingly small niche in the midst of nature's kingdom, they must take care to confine their own world and tread lightly in nature's. Evolution has created mountain wonderlands of plants and animals, but the high alpine ecosystems are fragile and rare. Short growing seasons and marginal conditions make life tenuous and recovery from disruption difficult. Human carelessness can destroy in a moment an ecological balance achieved over decades.

With luck and care, nature will remain so pure and awesome here that humans who venture into the mountains will carry away with them a sense of her beauty, power, fragility and importance. And, just as crucial, leave behind no trace of their own passing.

Panoramas and microcosms: A single yellow lily is one of the first flowers to greet the spring; wild sheep look down from rocky perches; lightning streaking the sky beyond dead trees creates a dramatic scene. Previous page: Dying sunlight tints the town and Paradise Divide in pastel pink and blue.

THE PEOPLE

STRONG WILLS, GENTLE SPIRITS

He covered the terrain, the terrain covered him. Jean Pavillard (left) grins at the finish of the Al Johnson Memorial Uphill/Downhill Telemark Race. He didn't win, but he did survive. Previous page: Mickey Cooper, Jennifer Gers, and Angela Hornwood strut their colors in the Mountain Theatre's 1989 production of "Jesus Christ Superstar."

Crested Butte's surrounding mountains dominate the camera lens with their commanding presence. But the town's people, outwardly unpretentious, emanate an equal, if more subtle, beauty.

Roughened by high-altitude sun, wind and dryness, and dressed in deference to nature rather than fashion, Crested Butte's people seldom bother to compete with the glamor of more affluent resort communities. But if these environs are cruel to skin and wardrobes, they are kind to hearts, and that kindness reflects back in faces that are friendly, unguarded and curious. Here the buildings wear false fronts, not the people.

Jack Blanton, who created the much-acclaimed Skyland Resort and Country Club, practices a putt at the championship golf course just south of Crested Butte. After many a missed putt, Blanton (who also built the Three Seasons building and started Trans-Colorado Airlines) was proclaimed a better visionary than golfer.

Biologists at the nearby Rocky Mountain Biological Laboratory have discovered several rare plants found only on certain area mountaintops, where they were stranded as the glaciers retreated 10,000 years ago. Similarly, Crested Butte, isolated in the mountains, preserves qualities rarely found in twentieth-century America. Trust, lack of fear, openness and caring still thrive. Hard work still accomplishes more than manipulative savvy. Honesty is still the best policy — since the neighbors will find out anyway. And if the local rumor mill gets a little over-productive, Crested Butte's general open-mindedness makes it more humorous than malicious.

True, this is no homogeneous population. The people range from corporate executives intent on thriving in a high-tech, highly competitive industry to oldtimers still loading coal into the cookstove. In between are families, retirees, young professionals, punksters, and ski bums from seventeen years to seventy. Spirited debates sometimes fill the town council chambers and editorial pages over how best to guide the town. But the people share an affection for Crested Butte and a determination to protect the quality of life here. Young and old are willing and proud to

Sandy Cortner and Tony Verzuh step lively around the dance floor during a Memorial Day polka. Polkas have been a central part of certain Crested Butte celebrations since the town's beginnings.

J ohn Rozman, Sr., and son Richard
take a lunch break while haying
their fields north of Crested Butte.
Despite some lean times for Colorado
ranchers, the Rozmans have ranched
their lands in the area for
generations.

Danica Ayraud (above) relishes her feline alter ego during the Stepping Stones carnival in Town Park. Bill Smith (right), a.k.a. the Doctor of Soot, pursues his mission of keeping the town "from making an ash of itself." Smith runs Chim Chimney Sweep and The Heating Source stove shop and makes cameo appearances in the town's parades disguised as — you guessed it — a chimney.

share Crested Butte and her mountains with those who show the same reverence for her. But threaten to abuse her, and watch out.

The oldtimers' claim on Crested Butte comes from decades of back-breaking work in harsh conditions. The town's first settlers, primarily Americans of English, Scotch and Irish ancestry, defied the weather, snow and isolation to seek their fortunes in the mineral-rich mountains. Around the turn of the century, mass migration from Central and Southern Europe brought hundreds of poor immigrants to the mountains looking for work. Crested Butte's mining labor force then included many Italians and a few Germans, but the people were mostly Croatians and Slovenes from Yugoslavia. The old family names in Crested Butte — Sporcich, Yelenick, Stefanic, Ruggera, Tezak, Somrak — and the

Perennial clown Nick Rayder brings smiles and mischief to the Fourth of July parade. Rayder, who commutes between California and Crested Butte, serves as college teacher and consultant for individual and organizational development — and occasional merry-maker.

Croatian lullabies that still sound out on Memorial Day show how those cultural roots continue.

The new immigrants faced not only the natural hardships, but exploitation by the mine bosses, some ethnic prejudice and sometimes unfamiliarity with the language as well. Gradually, some worked their way to positions of responsibility in the mines; others became shop owners in Crested Butte.

While the men developed stooped shoulders and black lung disease deep in the earth, the women kept the home fires burning, literally. On rare holidays, the people threw themselves into polkas, picnics and sledding parties as heartily as they toiled in the mines and homes. Plagues, mining disasters, and economic collapses drove away the weak of heart, and cemented the ties among those remaining.

As economics and logistics gradually closed the mines in the 1940s and '50s, the town's population dwindled to 200 or so. Still the town refused to die.

The seeds of tourism brought both hope and fear. The town's growing reputation as a mountain retreat drew a new breed of visitors and residents. In the '60s, long-haired young people in search of a purer lifestyle piled into the town's deserted, ramshackle buildings. One long-time resident said she slept with a gun by her bed when the grimy-looking strangers started moving to town. But history repeated itself, and

King Willard Ruggera and Queen Marlene Stajduhar celebrate their brief reign over Flauschink's end-of-winter craziness — before they're relegated to "Royal Has-Beens."

the heartiest new emigrants settled in, proved themselves hard workers and decent people, and, after lengthy battles in the council chambers and over backyard fences, the people forged a truce and entered the new era.

Now some of the ex-pony-tailed hippies own successful businesses and the battered Volkswagen buses were long ago traded for Broncos with baby seats. The oldtimers may still shake their head at the "frivolous" pastimes and New Age perspectives of the newer residents, but mutual respect and affection for the town helps maintain the bridge between them.

Unlike many old mining towns-turned-resorts whose buildings were resurrected while the old-time residents were chased away, Crested Butte still values its elders. The local youngsters trade Christmas gifts with the oldtimers, listen to their stories and grow to respect them. Vinotok, the Slavic fall festival started in 1984 to honor the elders, brings together all ages, from babes to octogenarians; and foot-tappers from all generations mix on the dance floor on Memorial Day when Chris Rouse strikes up a polka.

New waves of young people still roll into Crested Butte each winter, some to work a season and head back to college or mainstream job, some

The faces of the game: Hunter Dale (far left) keeps his cool despite the unfolding drama of local t-ball; a Gunnison youngster gives that ball his teeth-gritting best (below left); and Crested Butte t-ball coach Vic Shepard (below) counsels a disheartened Patrick Gillen.

Firefighters Lenny Zuehlke, Jeff Neumann, and Michael Helland study the behavior of a fire during a practice session (left). Above, John Holder and fellow emergency medical technicians home their skills in a staged rescue attempt. Crested Butte's well-trained volunteers get called away from work, sleep, even softball by the piercing town fire alarm — and the chorus of dogs that inevitably joins in.

*F*aces of Crested Butte: Kay
Peterson, local enchilada queen (part
owner of Donita's Cantina) and
mountain bike magnate (invincible
rider and organizer of Fat Tire Bike
Week); Scott Escott after a soggy fat
tire bike race up Paradise Divide;
and Bridger Smith, sinking his teeth
into a watermelon slice during a
backyard picnic.

to take root. Hacky-sack, rock and roll, and bumper-stickered Volkswagen vans will never die in Crested Butte, just get handed down from time to time.

Like in its earlier days, Crested Butte has become a family town. Mountain athletes still pound the ski slopes and visitors marvel at the energy and fitness of the townspeople. But some of the enthusiasm that twenty years ago went toward skiing and hallucinating has been rechanneled toward school board politics and Mountain Theatre productions; economic development and hospital fund-raising; preservation of the environment in the water courts and legislature. Mary Yelenick Park, one of the most child-pleasing playscapes in the county, came to life through donated goods and community labor. Three

Little angels, at least for the moment: Crested Butte Community School students chime out the music for the school's production of "Mary Poppins."

F*rank Yelenick, former miner and owner of Crested Butte Liquor, shares a warm hug with a young Paris Lumb, the daughter of Bakery Cafe owners Sam and Nan Lumb.*

S*inger, songwriter, and artist Tracey Wickland (top) has serenaded Crested Butte for years, on special occasions and at various nightspots around town. Mary Volk (lower), an almost-native of Crested Butte who works at the Crested Butte State Bank, celebrates Flauschink with friends at Kochevar's Bar.*

hundred people, about a quarter of the area population, worked together
for a solid weekend on behalf of the children.

Yet for all their changing, the people of Crested Butte still love a good
party (be it beer bash or school carnival), a good joke, and a good pair of
powder skis. And the town applauds its off-beat characters — bald-
pated Frog, fishman Botsie, flamboyant Bookie —as much as its more
conservative citizenry. So maybe the mountains can't protect people
from the cares of adulthood — but Crested Butte at least lets the child in
them come out a little more often and have a little more fun.

While year-round residents mind the store on a daily basis, Crested
Butte boasts a widespread network of honorary locals — second home

Crested Butte's schoolyard (above) turns into a sledding center after-hours. Left, Abigail Norton gives a side glance to her supporters on her way to the finish line of the sack race during the school's outdoor play day.

owners or just loyal fans — who give money, time and care to the town. For some "commuter locals," Crested Butte feels more like home than their own suburban neighborhoods, and they follow local events more closely than those living full-time within the town limits. Crested Butte's honorary locals have made possible some accomplishments the town could not have attained by itself; they donated most of the $500,000 raised to create the Center for the Performing Arts in 1987.

The people of Crested Butte can be tough and generous, good-humored and cantankerous, laid-back and energetic. They can feud and bicker, yet rally as one to fight a perceived threat or support a friend in need.

Many people nurture Crested Butte — no splashy superheroes here. The unsung heroes include people like octogenarian Tony Mihelich, who still runs the Conoco with quiet friendliness and the smile of a gentle saint. And Tuck, mountain man, karate instructor, actor, bus driver, horse wrangler and unwitting guru. And Glo Cunningham, boundless source of hugs and enthusiasm. And the late Mary Yelenick, long-time schoolteacher and shopkeeper who embraced everyone with equal kindness. The list goes on...no superstars, just strong, good-hearted people in a place that brings out their best.

C.M. Daniell (below), a former Texan who recently moved to Crested Butte, sips his morning coffee outside his store, Heartland, on Elk Avenue.

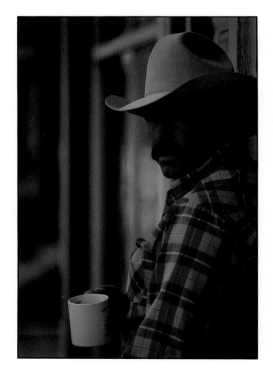

The Rozman brothers, Rudy and John (left), ride through the lush fields of the family ranch at the base of Whetstone Mountain south of Crested Butte.

Warmth, a la Crested Butte. Mary Yelenick (below), former schoolteacher and proprietress of Crested Butte Liquor, embraced everyone she met with open arms; after her death, the town proclaimed a day in her honor and named the new playscape in the Town Park after her. Mary's brand of love reflects back in the faces of youngsters like Amanda Wojtalik (left), peeking mischievously through mid-summer fireweed.

Newlyweds Glo Cunningham and Scott Wimmer, much-loved members of the community, evoked tears and cheers at their outdoor wedding during the summer of 1988.

The child-like curiosity hidden in people of all ages comes alive at the Rocky Mountain Biological Laboratory, where biologists and nature-lovers rekindle the urge to ask questions. Internationally renowned environmental biologist and author Paul Ehrlich (left) examines a butterfly caught in the field; students (right) gather like eager youngsters around a newfound discovery.

Crested Butte Mayor Mickey Cooper and Mt. Crested Butte Mayor Joe Fitzpatrick (top) dispose of the tedious duties of office (parade-sitting, picnic-going, autograph-signing, etc.) as The Mayor Brothers. You may have heard of them...
Joy McClure (lower) strikes a classic mid-winter pose. She's still smiling; either it's early in the winter, or she's got the day off and a ski pass tucked under her sweater.

NATHAN BILOW PHOTOGRAPHY

Nathan Bilow has become known internationally for his photographic ability to freeze a moment — ordinary or extraordinary, in the front yard or around the globe — so each viewer becomes part of the moment, its feeling and significance.

Photography has been second nature to Nathan since he got a hand-me-down camera at age five. Over the years, relatives gave him old college books and cast-off cameras, and he started a lawn mowing service to afford film. "As I got better jobs, I got better gear," he said.

During high school in Southern California, Nathan set up a lab, and after graduation shot upcoming Hollywood stars for a modeling agency.

Despite early setbacks (the camera gear he'd tied to his wrist while camping on the beach was cut loose and stolen during a nine-month trip in Europe), Nathan persevered.

In the late '70s, he bought some winter clothes ("I'd *heard* of long underwear") and moved to Colorado. In Crested Butte, Nathan traded work for lodging at the Niccolis' ranch, learning about animals, "good old country people," and baking bread in a coal stove. Gradually he began taking photos again, doing lab and photography work for the local newspapers, and his excitement about photography was rekindled.

When the Associated Press wire service used a shot of Nathan's from the Chronicle, the door to the big time opened. Nathan became a regular photographer for AP, and quickly was accepted into national ranks. Ski Magazine hired him to shoot the North Face in 1982 and his work has since appeared in hundreds of international media, including Sports Illustrated, Sailing, Outside, New York Times, Powder and Bicycling.

Several stock agencies represent Nathan,

and he spends six to nine months a year traveling on assignment and for his own stock. His travels have taken him to Mexico, Canada, Europe, Hawaii, Alaska, Central America, New Zealand, the South Pacific, New Caledonia, Oman, and most of the United States.

What makes a good photographer? "Being able to see something special in what the normal person takes for granted, and to capture it on film," Nathan said. "It's taking the right time to shoot, shooting action, then reaction. It's smiles and sadness. It's what life is about."

Nathan relishes the challenge of international photography, capturing such diverse moods as a quaint French village and the colorful action of sailors "beating the wind."

"I want people to react to my pictures,

no matter what it is — action, sad, happy — and to put themselves within that, so the viewer can be part of the reality I've had."

No one stays inside during the enticing days of summer and the Town Park becomes an informal social center. For youngsters, the park hosts t-ball and softball and provides an imaginative playscape, the Mary Yelenick Park. For older players, the park offers softball, soccer, tennis, horseshoes and volleyball. Some folks play; others cheer, heckle, or distribute libations. Tom Stillo (right) earns himself major points for form, style and effort for his volleyball heroics — whether he got the ball back over the net or not.

THE LIFESTYLE

COLD FEET, WARM HEARTS

July, 1980. Conversation overheard in the newly-snowed-on garden:

Q. "So do you think this is the last snow of last winter or the first snow of next winter?"

A. (Slightly sullen) "Who cares?"

Over the years, various humans have officially governed Crested Butte, but everyone knows who really rules here: that matriarch Mother Nature and her tyrannical sidekick, Old Man Winter.

Nature gives the other seasons their token turns; summer's rainbow hues and autumn's fiery plumage make up in brilliance what they lack in longevity. But anyone planning to live happily in Crested Butte had best make their peace first with the neighborhood bully, winter.

To be fair, Old Man Winter gives the town its ski slopes, toboggan runs, white Christmases, and romantic picturescapes. And all the townspeople have to do in return is occasionally man the hair dryer to thaw the pipes; maneuver their vehicles over ice-coated mountain roads while pretending they're fully in control; shovel snow and chop wood long after the novelty has worn off; figure out where to stash the car so the snowplow won't remodel it; and experiment with various contortions trying to get the feet warm in bed without having to get up and put wool socks on. And, hey, one perfect day of skiing fresh powder can erase a whole week's worth of such minor hassles.

To hear the locals talk, Crested Butte has an eight-month winter and a seven-month economy. Nobody gets rich; everybody gets chill bumps. So why does this place grab hold of people so tenaciously? Why do the families that move to greener urban pastures so often scurry back?

Maybe there's something a bit addictive about feeling you can be yourself, dress as you want, leave the doors unlocked, escape easily into the wilderness by foot, ski or bike, and live among people who appreciate beauty, nature, and each other.

Tom Gifford (below), local painter who introduced purple as a mainstay of Crested Butte's color scheme, jazzes up another building.

Tony Mihelich preserves a timeless world, the Conoco station and Crested Butte Hardware Store. The inside of the building has not been altered since the turn of the century.

Crested Butte at work: Lee Dickelman (top) running the kitchen of his Paradise Cafe (a.k.a. Lee's Leisure Dome); Nadine Israel (bottom) hawking Crested Butte as the former director of the Crested Butte/Mt. Crested Butte Chamber of Commerce; and ski instructor Lisa Straubhaar (far right) riding the lift with two eager young students.

Maybe doing without that new car is an acceptable sacrifice for living in a place where trust and friendliness aren't squelched by fear. Chief Marshal Rich Largo sounds far from a big-city cop when he comments, "I hire officers who believe people are basically good and worthy of respect; I think that reflects Crested Butte. That approach might not work in Chicago, but it works here. We don't have many bad people here; when they move to town, they show up right away."

Now, various locals have sarcastically speculated that Crested Butte stays such an idyllic haven because money, the reputed source of all evil, remains such a scarce commodity here. Although Gunnison County was rated one of the ten most highly-educated counties in the United States, Crested Butte's residents sometimes take jobs they haven't worked since high school just to live here. And while the area's growing economy is allowing ever-increasing numbers of people to find professionally

Crested Butte at play: Catch some reggae at the ElDorado, rock and roll at Rafters, or boogie to the dolstrum at the Talk of the Town. The dolstrum? Not your typical ski resort fare, perhaps, but Jean-Paul Simille and Mary Jo Somrak seem to be getting a kick out of Edyth Bauer's lively polkas.

*C*rested Butte at home: Houses range from simple shelters like the teepee below, at one time a popular summer housing option; to quaint downtown houses like the two huddling together at the corner of First and Elk (David Sumner's house on the left has since been torn down); to the exotic and luxurious "clamshell house" (right) tucked into an aspen grove on the slopes of Mt. Crested Butte.

satisfying positions, the pay usually pales compared to similar jobs in the city.

So, unlike their urban counterparts, Crested Butte's people more often center their lives and egos around their true passions — skiing, biking, climbing, kayaking, suntanning — rather than their jobs. Some take this to the extreme, waiting tables every winter and summer to finance autumn's adventuring in Nepal, Yosemite, Africa, or their own backyard. To someone prone to hanging by his fingertips 1500 feet up a sheer rock face, long-term security can seem an irrelevant concern.

Others drift toward more traditional lifestyles, trading some of their freedom and adrenaline rushes for business ownership, demanding professions or parenthood. But they're still in Crested Butte; the closet still has more t-shirts than button-downs and the skis, however cob-webbed, stand in the corner, just in case. And Crested Butte's beauty and quality of life continue to influence their lives, however subliminally.

Whatever a person's occupation and enthusiasm level in December, late March inevitably sows the seeds of discontent. This comes partly from cabin fever and partly from the nature of the jobs around here,

Crested Butte Mountain Resort has forged its niche in a competitive ski industry through state-of-the-art operations, marketing and sales. Rick Jernigan, vice president for resort services, and Tom Shepard, senior vice president for mountain operations (right), are forced to ski almost daily in the course of their work. Ski Patrol members (top, far right) survey avalanche paths during their early-morning rounds. Ralph Walton (nicknamed Bubba), chairman of the board for CBMR, beams behind the sign at Bubba's, the restaurant named in his honor (below, far right).

*S*now, the charm and the callouses: Joe
Fitzpatrick and son (left) conjure romantic
images as they trek into the countryside to
fetch the family Christmas tree. The guy
shoveling the roof of the old powerhouse
building (above) is perhaps not so charmed.
With twenty-five feet or so of snow each year,
Crested Butte satiates the greediest of snow-
lovers by the time summer finally arrives.

which are primarily tourist- and service-oriented. As a whole, Gunnison County's economy rests on three pillars — tourism, ranching and education. While Western State College in Gunnison (28 miles south of Crested Butte) recently has enjoyed increased enrollment and upgraded academic standards, and the beleaguered ranchers are feeling an economic upswing, tourism far outweighs the other economies. Ranchers around Crested Butte — mostly the Rozman, Veltri, Niccoli and Eccher families — still drive their cattle along the highway to and from the highlands and are very much a part of the land, tradition and economy. But tourism now keeps the town alive.

Most locals, then, make a living by luring visitors to this mountain playground and helping them enjoy it. Not a bad job description, theoretically. But when showing them a good time includes scrubbing their cold, greasy breakfast plates, well...

By April, almost every job is wearing thin and employees resort to creative methods of releasing tension and maintaining perspective — bashing the moguls, planning mud season escapades, or donning outlandish get-ups and bizarre alter egos for the Red Lady Ball, Flauschink, the Marmots and various beach and costume parties. A few springs ago, a ski shop supervisor found his employees, an exceptionally gregarious and good-natured crew, making little rag effigies of the season's most obnoxious customers and gleefully torturing them with a propane torch. Time for vacation.

Like boot camp, the lifestyle in Crested Butte builds strength, of body and will. The town has become known for its exceptionally strong and co-supportive women, some of whom can chop and haul wood, raise children, make a living, ski and bike, shovel the roof, and hunt for wild game with the best. Former newspaper editor Paul Andersen once affectionately described Crested Butte as a town "where the men are men and the women are, too." (The gentleman, it is rumored, had just been beaten up the hill by a member of the gentler sex during a grueling bike ride.)

Kids, too, have it pretty rough in Crested Butte. Deprived of huge shopping malls and video arcades, they resort to strange behaviors like talking to each other and using their imaginations. Without a lot of expensive school equipment, they have to settle for creative, dedicated teachers and involved community members for their education.

With little crime or traffic and plenty of playmates, Crested Butte lets kids enjoy being kids. The photo of Bridger Smith (left) riding his scooter down the sidewalk on Elk Avenue bespeaks the simple, carefree days childhood should be made of. For hard-working families like Joel and M.J. Vosburg and their son Zachary (above), respite from the rat race waits just outside the back door.

He's humble; he's a pacifist; he's a much-loved fifty year old with grandkids. He's also a black belt in karate, Mountain Theatre performer, horse wrangler, and the hottest ticket going for spicing up a bachelorette party. Yep, it's Tuck (top). Below, Peter Muller brightens Crested Butte's wardrobe with his splashy and practical sportswear, made and sold through his *Pro Leisure* shop.

Susan Anderton (above) paints a new Mountain Express bus. The six buses, each painted in 1983 by a different local artist as part of a cooperative arts project, provide moving works of art while transporting residents and guests between Crested Butte and the ski area. Jim Mayfield (below), owner of Colorado Boomerangs, stands behind colorful, freshly-painted boomerangs in his Gunnison workshop.

Morning dew and sunlight dramatize an everyday summer flowerscape. Previous page: Herschel Augspurger plays Pontius Pilate in the Mountain Theatre's "Jesus Christ Superstar"; Pitsker Sporcich, a young apple lover, and Jennifer Gers enjoy a warm afternoon on Elk Avenue.

Strangely enough, the kids not only survive, but grow into unusually independent, expressive and confident young people — and often exceptional skiers.

With Mother Nature being so heavy-handed here, Crested Butte's humans march to seasonal rhythms as dutifully as their wildlife neighbors do. Autumn sends everyone — fly, sparrow, marmot and sales clerk — into a frenzy, feeding, scavenging, or scouring the classifieds for jobs or housing. Winter starts out inspirationally beautiful, tempting novitiates to ski like crazy, work like crazy, celebrate like crazy, and collapse long before the party's over. Then, it's hang in there till spring — muddy, quiet, glorious spring. Time of siesta, snowpits, and mass

exodus to points south. Then — ah — summer. Crested Butte's summer mimics those shopping sprees on television where some lucky winner is turned loose in a grocery store for sixty seconds to scramble for all the goods he or she can pile up. For the few short, idyllic weeks of summer, Mother Nature invites recreationists into her flower-carpeted playground to see how much fun they can have, how many images and tales they can collect before the aspens gleam golden and the snows close in.

Yes, life in Crested Butte remains amazingly devoid of pretense, status-obsession, crime, and other urban by-products, but perhaps the townspeople shouldn't take too much credit; maybe they're just too busy trying to keep ahead of winter to be tempted by such distractions.

Jennifer Elenbaas and Kris Kerbel, students in the Crested Butte School of Dance, create points of light on a summer landscape.

111

Christy Best and Frank Orazem warm the bench outside Frank's home on Elk Avenue. After Frank, a gentle and big-hearted native of Crested Butte, died in 1986, his grave was appropriately marked with a giant wooden heart he had made from a curved tree trunk.

WESTERN STATE COLLEGE

Western State College promises "an education to match our mountains"; but it also delivers education to match the students. With small classes, personal counseling, high teacher-to-student ratio and flexible course planning, WSC allows students to tailor their own education.

Besides the college's personal approach, WSC's strength lies partly in a recognition that some of the best learning takes place outside the classroom walls. With the college's own resources on campus (radio and television studios, theatres, biofeedback and other labs, art gallery and recital halls) and the setting in nature's expansive "outdoor laboratory," WSC provides early hands-on experience for students. Professors in fields such as art, biology, environmental sciences, geology, history, photography and recreation use the mountain setting to teach and inspire.

Traditional academic work is also supplemented by extracurricular activities ranging from skiing (with a national-calibre ski team) and other sports, to the highly-respected WSC Mountain Rescue Team, to theatre and music groups, to award-winning student media. The Wilderness Pursuits program brings students into the mountains, sharpening skills, confidence and awareness.

Approximately 2,400 students study 21 disciplines at WSC. At 7,735 feet elevation, WSC is higher than any other four-year college in the country, and one of the oldest on Colorado's Western Slope. The school was founded in 1911 as a "normal school" to prepare teachers who would educate the children of Colorado's isolated communities. Renamed a decade later and expanded into a general liberal arts and sciences college,

WSC now emphasizes "the education of adaptable, multidisciplined graduates." WSC alumni have distinguished themselves in many diverse fields.

The college and the home community of Gunnison (population 5,000) provide a warm environment for students. A 1980 census rated Gunnison County the eighth-best-educated county in the nation, yet it remains homey and comfortable. As one college representative wrote, "Almost without exception, our graduates leave this valley with a special affection for the community and its people. Many of the local residents — almost one in ten — are former students who came to study, liked what they found, and stayed."

WSC's alumni are unusually loyal to the school, offering the college and the students a continual helping hand. Roxanne Bradshaw, WSC graduate who serves as secretary/treasurer for the National Education Association, commented on the close bonds that form at the college: "I've found the mentor system which develops at a small campus — coupled with a faculty philosophy of care and concern — has given me a supportive network which is still a vital part of my professional success."

Recently, WSC has seen upgraded academic standards and increased enrollment. But the college remains committed to the small, personal scale and hands-on approach to education.

RECREATION

WILD PLAYGROUNDS

Crested Butte began its life as a hub for miners crawling around the mountains in search of mineral riches. Today, Crested Butte earns its livelihood as a base for recreationists riding, skiing and hiking the same mountains in search of more modern bounty — beauty and adventure.

While many of yesteryear's prospectors left the mountains weary and empty-handed, today's mountain explorers inevitably return home refreshed and satiated. Mother Nature hid her minerals, but beauty and adventure she splashed generously throughout the mountains.

Will he make it? Harold Johnson decides to go for it at the icy creek crossing on the 1986 Pearl Pass Tour. He's smiling, but onlookers suspect his teeth are clenched behind that grin. Previous page: Even from the back, this airborne skier looks like he's having fun.

No engineer could have designed a more complete recreational mecca. Dependable, heavy snowfalls, frequent sunshiny weather, and varied ski terrain tempt skiers of all persuasions, telemark or alpine, track or cross-country, in the backcountry or at the resort. Open valleys leading upward to rugged mountainsides offer every type of mountain

*N*o, *they're not on the North Face, Phoenix Bowl or Banana chutes. But Steve "Bones" Gerner and Steve Griffith can make skiing look like an adventure even on the gentle rolls of Paradise Bowl.*

biking, from gentle roads to radically steep trails. Run-off streams offer chilly thrills to boaters and fishing challenges for beginners or fanatics.

With four wilderness areas surrounding Crested Butte, backpackers and others who venture off the beaten path can find rare solitude and peace. But for those who like their recreation a bit more refined, one of the finest high-altitude golf courses in the country nestles at the base of Crested Butte Mountain. And Crested Butte offers all the classic vacation amenities — tennis, racquetball, swimming, and athletic club facilities.

By land, Crested Butte also offers extensive horseback riding, carriage and sleigh rides, walking tours, rock climbing, educational programs at the Rocky Mountain Biological Lab, snowmobiling, jeeping, kayaking, dog sledding, softball and volleyball, toboganning, shopping, music, art and theatre, and some of the finest dining in the state. By air, people can view the mountains from a hot air balloon, or sail their hang-gliders off Crested Butte Mountain, widely recognized as a premier, advanced hang-gliding site. Yet, with all that, the area remains beautiful and pristine, with no crowds, traffic, or extravagant price tags.

Among mountain bike enthusiasts, Crested Butte remains the undisputed mecca, with good reason. Not only do the surrounding mountains and valleys create limitless spectacular rides, but fat tire bikes made their comeback via the town.

Recreation, refined or rugged: The John Jacobs Practical Golf School hosts the LPGA golf tour (far left) at Skyland Country Club; mountain bikers (left) choose backcountry mud over country club greens during this snowy Pearl Pass Tour.

Miquel Llonch and Mireia Garcia (above) hike along a lush waterfall north of Crested Butte. On a single hike, backpackers may encounter tropical-looking scenes like this and huge snowfields still prime for skiing. Back in civilization, Paul Hird (right) stretches for a backhand shot at Skyland's tennis court.

Twenty years ago, fat tire bikes in Crested Butte meant resurrected old one-speed klunkers, the only bikes that could withstand the town's potholed streets. As Crested Butte's klunker-riders were taking their ancient wrecks ever farther into the mountains, some crazy Californians were experimenting with beefing up the fat-tired bikes with multiple speeds and lightweight components. With a little cross-breeding, the high-tech mountain bike and a rapidly growing sport were born.

Today, many locals still ride battered one-speed "town bikes" for transportation, but almost every household has its high-tech mountain bikes for more radical entertainment. Meanwhile, visiting mountain bikers come from all over the country, from hardcore "pedalheads" to family tourers. Fat Tire Bike Week brings together several hundred industry reps, competitors, adventurers and low-key recreationists for tours, races and social events. And the famous Pearl Pass Tour from

F*at Tire Bike Week in 1989 drew almost a thousand fat tire fans for scenic tours, serious competition and socializing. Above, riders line up on Elk Avenue for the start of the Pearl Pass Tour in 1988, when the tour was still part of Fat Tire Bike Week. The following year, FTBW was moved to July, but the Pearl Pass Tour stayed in September. Somehow the possibility of riding through snow flurries seemed central to the Pearl Pass Tour tradition.*

As *part of Fat Tire Bike Week's most colorful event, the mountain bike rodeo, Peter Delaney (above) concentrates on getting small in the limbo contest and another competitor contorts his face with effort in the log-pulling contest (left).*

Crested Butte to Aspen continues each autumn, building on a tradition more than 15 years old.

In 1975, a group of Aspenites rode their motorcycles over Pearl Pass to Crested Butte. Not to be outdone, a small contingent of hearty Crested Butte riders bounced, battled and carried their one-speed klunkers back over the pass to Aspen. The Pearl Pass Tour gradually became an institution, with as many as 300 riders tackling the tough 30-mile ride.

As with biking and, well, almost everything, Crested Butte's young people didn't settle for the mainstream approach to skiing either. Many skiers 15 years ago skied more in the backcountry than at the ski area. To combine easier access to the backcountry with the thrill of downhill skiing, ski patrolman Rick Borkovec and compatriots re-invented the old telemark turn from pictures of skiers around the turn of the century.

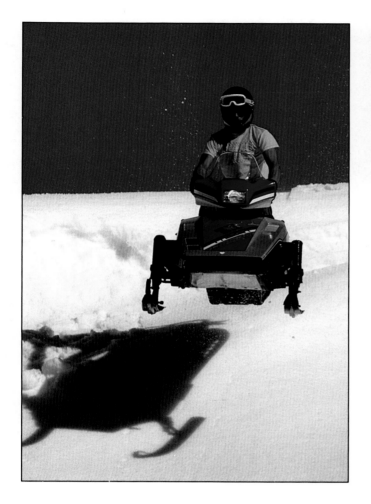

The swooping telemark turn allowed downhill skiing on cross-country equipment. Today, telemarking has become a sport unto itself, and the skis have become so specialized that skiers often buy different skis for powder snow and for groomed slopes. For local skiers, telemarking still represents another on-slope challenge, added versatility, rebellion against the snowplowing masses, and a sort of local trademark. Some tele-converts have defected back to their alpine skis, but Crested Butte still boasts a loyal contingent of telemarking die-hards.

Always quick to embrace the off-beat, Crested Butte has also become a hot spot for snowboarding and various other methods of propelling oneself down a snowy slope at high speed. Also, the Irwin Lodge, high in the Ruby Range west of Crested Butte, offers the one of the largest snowcat/helicopter skiing operations in the country.

There's more than one way to play on snow. Du and Bugs DuVal (left) share obvious delight in their innertube race; John Biro of Burt Rentals Snowmobile Tours (center) goes for max air off a cornice near Lake Irwin; and a snowboarder (left) tries out new antics on the half-pipe at the ski resort.

Fishing for solitude, challenge, or dinner. Bill Clapet and Amanda Wojtalik (left) test the waters at Lake Irwin; Betsy Heartfield (right) meets with more humor than success in her fly-tying attempts; and Don Mills (below) shows off a whopper he snagged in Blue Mesa Reservoir.

In Crested Butte, temptation comes
in many forms — inviting
nightspots, unusual shops and
enticing eateries like Soupcon,
Penelope's and the Bakery Cafe,
pictured at right.

After a tough day on the slopes, recreationists find a varied menu of food and entertainment in Crested Butte. Despite its small size, down-home style, and rustic appearance, the town has become famous for its sophistication. M. Carlton of the *Denver Post* credited the town with having "more fine restaurants per capita than any other town in the America." Ambience ranges from elegant to splintery, with entrees from duck to pizza.

After dinner, those with energy left can often catch live music or a Mountain Theatre production during the peak times of the year. The longest-running community theatre in Colorado, the Mountain Theatre showcases the amazing talent tucked away in Crested Butte; volunteers donate numberless hours to create sets, costumes, lighting effects and sometimes daring productions that delight their audiences.

As if the daily fare weren't enough, Crested Butte spices the calendar liberally with special events. During the winter, fund-raisers for cystic fibrosis research and physically challenged skiers bring celebrities and hoopla to town. The Subaru U.S. Alpine Championships draw the best young alpine ski racers in the country, along with widespread media coverage. In contrast, the relatively obscure Al Johnson Memorial Uphill/Downhill draws an irreverent group of the country's top telemarkers for one of the wildest ski races around; skiers scramble like

penquins up a steep slope, then fly 1200 vertical feet down the expert terrain of the North Face. In similar spirit, the Alley Loop nordic race leads all levels of cross-country skiers through Crested Butte's downtown streets and alleys, where they're cheered on by spectators in backyard snowpits and lawn chairs.

As winter wears on and cabin fever threatens, the celebrations take on a touch of frenzy. The High Country Citizens Alliance's Red Lady Ball with its annual dance contest inspires bizarre costumes and matching

Michael Helland and his sons, Jesse and Cam (far left), scout the forest for game in preparation for hunting season. Jim Talbot (left) leads an overnight pack trip from Crested Butte to Aspen.

High in the Rockies: After launching off Crested Butte Mountain, this hang-glider (far left) gets a bird's eye view of the town. Backpackers Bob Wojtalik and Larry Hansen had to work a bit harder to gain altitude, but the rewards are obvious. On a snowy summit, Larry (below) takes a moment for introspection and journal-writing.

Same sport, different feelings: Competitors in the Alley Loop nordic race (right) skate along Crested Butte's alleys and side streets, cheered on by backyard spectators; Gail Burford and Monty Huntington (top, far right) carve their telemark skis gracefully through fresh powder; and a high-speed downhill racer (bottom, far right) edges around a gate in pursuit of title and prize money in the prestigious Subaru U.S. Alpine Championships held in Crested Butte every year.

behavior. April also brings the Golden Marmots, the Mountain Theatre's slightly tongue-in-cheek answer to the Academy Awards and an excuse to trade a winter's worth of longjohns and parkas for sequins and silk (perhaps topped off with flashy red high-tops).

Summer officially opens with Memorial Day, a time for family reunions and solemnity in the cemetery, followed by a rollicking polka for all ages downtown. The Butte celebrates Independence Day with an old-fashioned Fourth, complete with homegrown parade and street games like the dog/owner look-alike contest and log-sawing races. Throughout July, wildflower and photography workshops take students into fields rich with color and life. The Arts Fair, a renowned, juried festival that draws hundreds of top level artists and thousands of spectators, turns Elk Avenue into a carnival of art, music, food and dance. Then Aerial Weekend paints the skies, with brilliant hot air balloons, hang-gliders, stunt pilots, parachutists, and kites and games in the park. As the shadows grow longer and coolness tinges September's breezes, Vinotok brings the community together for storytelling, wine and beer tasting, lamb roast, polka, procession and bonfire.

It's true, Crested Butte lacks the seductive bright lights and man-made amusements of the big city. But Crested Butte specializes in its own brand of celebration and recreation. A spirit of playfulness pervades the town and the invitation to play comes in 14,000-foot-high packages. Whether you wield a croquet mallet or ice axe, credit card or carabiners, that invitation can be hard to resist.

The goal is the finish line, but the purpose is fun. Andy Shepard and Ian Joyner (left) look more intent on staying vertical than on winning the three-legged race during the Crested Butte Community School playday. For top Munsingwear racer Ned Overend (above), the stakes and the intensity are a little higher.

To each his own mode of fun:
Morning sun rouses campers (left)
who'll spend the day on a wild ride
into Aspen as part of the Pearl Pass
Tour; Patty O'Brien (top right)
lunges for a backhand shot during a
match at Skyland Country Club; and
Inga Benedict (bottom right) leads
the pack during the Munsingwear
bike race in Mt. Crested Butte.

Miquel Llonch flies off a steep roll in the ski area's Extreme Limits. On purpose.

CRESTED BUTTE MOUNTAIN RESORT

Crested Butte Mountain Resort several years ago drew national attention when its ads proclaimed, "Heaven Forbid We Should Ever Be Like Aspen or Vail." The slogan said a lot about Crested Butte; its use by CBMR said a lot about the ski company.

CBMR prides itself on adopting the best of modern ski trends without losing the spirit of the town or the sport. While other resorts have tamed and packaged skiing for mass appeal, Crested Butte has introduced some of the most daring ski terrain in the country, the expert-only North Face. And while competing with other areas in vacation amenities such as child care, restaurants and ski instruction, Crested Butte remains a community as much as a resort. Vacationers become Crested Butte's personal guests, and often its friends.

Author and extreme skier Lito Tejada-Flores described Crested Butte as "one of the most vital small towns in the Rockies with the finest adventure skiing in Colorado." He credited Crested Butte Mountain Resort with "vision and commitment, two commodities not always in abundant supply in a ski industry progressively terrorized by the threat of lawsuits from skiers who want to be protected from their own lack of judgment."

Until a few years ago, adrenaline junkies had to hike for twenty minutes to reach the ungroomed powder stashes of the North Face and Phoenix Bowl. In 1987, the resort decided to access the steep, rugged terrain with a two-minute surface lift, yet maintain the area's wild, backcountry character. Adventurous skiers can now find untamed powder skiing filled with chutes, rolls, trees and other surprises — unlike any other lift-serviced skiing in Colorado.

While powderhounds revel in the the North Face, other skiers can find their own brand of fun — more than 800 acres of gentle beginner slopes, wide bowls, glades, moguls and steeps.

In addition to its extreme skiing, Crested Butte is also known throughout the industry for its innovative ski school. Founded two decades ago by Robel Straubhaar (named Colorado's ski instructor of the year in 1988), the ski school incorporates concepts such as breathing, relaxation and body awareness. Youngsters also find specially-tailored ski and snow games through the Children's Ski Center.

Despite its down-home character, Crested Butte has earned a reputation among the country's top ski racers as well, for its staging of America's highest-level national ski competition, the Subaru U.S. Alpine Championships presented by American Airlines.

Since its beginning in 1961, the Crested Butte ski area has grown from a tiny mom-and-pop ski hill to one of the top ten ski resorts in the state, and one of the fastest growing. It has grown not by commercializing the sport, but by offering a warm host community, a spectacular setting, and skiing as bold and varied as its visitors and locals demand.

THE TIMES

LOOKING BACK, LOOKING FORWARD

Mountains rise dramatically around the town of Mt. Crested Butte, dwarfing the luxurious Grande Butte Hotel and other modern shopping, dining and lodging facilities. Previous page: A detail of the Old Town Hall in Crested Butte shows how little some of the town's landmarks have changed in the past century.

If one of Crested Butte's early-day miners were to come stomping down out of the mountains today, he'd stop dead in his boots at the first signs of civilization. Hot pink and purple buildings, young people zipping past in skin-tight lycra, hot tubs and snowmaking machines...all visions beyond the imagination. But if he stopped in at Kochevar's to down a brew with the locals gathered there, he'd sense perhaps some threads unchanged from the town's rough beginnings.

True, every complaint these days about scratching for a living comes balanced by the commitment to protect the quality of life and the mountains and keep the twenty-first century at arm's length.

A mixing of old and new:
Animated Flauschink celebrants
(above) toast the newly-crowned
King and Queen at Kochevar's Bar.
The bar is turn-of-the-century
vintage; Flauschink's spring tradition
started in the late 60s; and the
revelers span several decades in age.

A century ago, when the only connection between snowbound Crested Butte and the outside world was a coal train, nobody worried about the potential evils of civilization. Nature, who vented her fury at will on hapless human beings, certainly needed no protection from them. And the lifestyle today, with its snowplows and electric heaters, might seem pretty soft to a man who spent twelve hours a day underground hacking at rock just to keep the family fed and clothed.

Still, the oldtimer might note, the people show some of the same camaraderie and spirit found among the townspeople in Crested Butte's early days. And there's still snow to shovel, pipes to thaw, and brews to share, just like in 1890. Compared to their urban peers, Crested Butte's people these days work hard, play hard, and pinch pennies, continuing a tradition as old as the town.

Never a flashy, affluent town, Crested Butte has always endured environmental and economic hardships through perseverence, heartiness and humor. Its wealth has always been in the hearts of its people rather than in its coffers.

Ironically, wealth, or the lust for it, gave birth to Crested Butte. It took rumors of gold to bring the first white men to the high, rugged Elk Mountains in the 1860s. Instead of riches, most of those early fortune-seekers found brutal weather and Ute Indians violently protective of their lands. The Utes massacred twelve white men in Washington Gulch and seven in Deadmans Gulch. Still, the dream of wealth was as compelling as life in the mountains was harsh and dreamers continued pushing little by little into the high country. The Utes were eventually given land on Kebler Pass, but the promise was revoked when valuable minerals were found there. White men had laid their claim on the valley.

Geologist Ferdinand Hayden unwittingly named Crested Butte on a surveying expedition in the Elk Mountains in 1873. From the top of Mt. Teocalli, he noted two rugged peaks standing alone (now Gothic and Crested Butte Mountain) and called them "the crested buttes." Crested Butte Mountain soon officially took the name, as did the town when it was formed several years later.

Tales of huge bituminous coal deposits in the Elk Mountains lured Howard F. Smith, now called "the father of Crested Butte," to the area in 1877. A partner in a smelting company in Leadville, Smith scouted the area briefly, then bought up most of the coal land along Coal Creek. By

Ethan Hicks and Gail Burford (below) enjoy the benefits of living in a small, rustic community with a major ski resort in the backyard.

CF&I company housing made up
much of the town in the early
twentieth century, as these row
houses (with their row outhouses)
illustrate. The large building on the
right is now the Elk Mountain
Lodge. Many of the company houses
have been moved or torn down; a
trailer park now occupies the land at
the left. Photo provided by the
Colorado Historical Society.

the summer of 1878, he had laid out the town of Crested Butte and helped build a sawmill. As silver camps and mines grew around the new town, the sawmill and smelter earned Crested Butte its role as a mining hub.

In his comprehensive history book, **The Gunnison Country** (which provided most of the following information on Crested Butte's early days), Western State College historian Duane Vandenbusche records a visitor's comments on early Crested Butte: "Every road leading out of town comes out before long in a mining camp. It is thus a natural center for supplies, and has in that one fact alone an excellent reason for being."

Crested Butte was officially incorporated on July 3, 1880. Smith was the first mayor of the town, which boasted a population of four hundred, with another thousand miners living within a three-mile radius. The town had fifty business houses, dwelling and tents, a smelter, three sawmills and the impressive Forest Queen House.

Rough and sometimes rowdy in its first years, the town vibrated with the hopes of fortune-seekers. But the rich veins of precious minerals remained elusive, with boom towns sprouting up and shriveling into ghost towns within a few decades.

While silver and gold ran their boom-and-bust cycles, coal — both bituminous and anthracite — remained Crested Butte's stable foundation for many decades. Much of the area coal also made high-quality coke. At first, along Coal Creek, workers dug tunnels into the exposed coal banks and cars carried the coal down to level ground to be burned by little piles into coke. By 1884, 154 beehive coke ovens made of fire brick and encased with stone were burning on the southern edge of Crested Butte.

The quality of the coke helped convince the Denver and Rio Grande Railroad to extend the rails to Crested Butte. On November 21, 1881, the first D&RG train rumbled into town, heralding an era of prosperity for the mines. Crested Butte's population reached its all-time high in the early 1880s with 1500 residents and by 1882 the town had five hotels, one bank, a dozen saloons, three livery stables, a dozen restaurants, five sawmills, two doctors, numberless lawyers, and a telephone line to Gunnison.

But like most coal towns of the times, Crested Butte was dirty, smelly, and gloomy. Mine owners intent on the bounty underground cut down trees, polluted the streams, and filled the air with coal dust. The sight

The Elk Mountain House held its grand opening in February 1892 with a lavish dinner and grand ball. Built by the town company, the impressive three-story hotel was one of the grandest hotels in the region. Colorado Historical Society photo.

dismayed newcomers traveling to the mountains to carve out a life for themselves and their families.

The earliest miners were Anglo-Saxons from Cornwall, Wales, Scotland, Germany and Ireland, where they had grown up with coal mines. After the mid-1890s, however, the town became home to many Slavic and Italian immigrants, arriving almost penniless, often unable to speak English and unfamiliar with mining. Ethnic disputes over religion, jobs, intermarriage and social status flared at first, but hardships drew the community together and dimmed ethnic differences.

While the surrounding mountains looked like heaven to those who had come from similar mountainous country in southern Europe, the living conditions were hellish. While the men burned themselves out underground, the women struggled to hold together households in the snowy, cold, isolated town. The mine companies badly exploited the workers, through meager wages, long hours deep below the Earth's surface, and inhuman working conditions. Besides the back-breaking, dirty work, dangerous conditions in the mines led to many deaths through fires, explosions, avalanches and other accidents. Almost every family lost a loved one through mining tragedies, the worst of which shocked the entire state.

The Jokerville Mine, opened just west of town in late 1881, was quickly labeled dangerous because of the excessive gas inside. An explosion in 1883 killed one miner and badly burned six others. But despite the warning signs, the company kept working the mine, halted only by the tragic mining disaster of 1884. Early on one cold January morning, a blast at the Jokerville shook the whole town. The explosion had destroyed one hundred feet of the frame tipple leading into the mine and smashed one of the ventilation fans. Fire raged in several buildings around the mine and blasted from the mine entrance.

The ensuing hours brought panic, hope, and finally tragedy, as historian Vandenbushe described: "Inside the hell below, those still alive scrambled frantically for the mine entrance...John Cashion kept his head and started leading his men toward the opening a third of a mile away. All felt their way along, stumbling over rocks, timbers, cars, coal, and the corpses of their fellow miners. It was a heartbreaking, ghastly, terrifying trip. Miraculously, after a half hour of groping along, the men reached the entrance and came out into the open. A tremendous cheer

Immigrants like those pictured above right poured into Crested Butte in the early 1900s; this photo was taken in Crested Butte around 1908. In the lower photo, chickens scratch around the tracks of the railroad depot, where D&RG trains carrying coal and passengers ran until the middle of the twentieth century. The tracks were pulled up after the Big Mine closed in 1952; the depot now serves as a community meeting center and houses the town's public library. Photo provided by the Colorado Historical Society.

went up from the waiting citizens of Crested Butte. Perhaps the other men trapped in the fiery hell in the mountain might also make their way out! Alas, it proved a false hope."

It took more than a week to retrieve all sixty corpses. A coroner's jury concluded the explosion had been caused by carbureted gas contacting naked light; apparently, it said, someone had entered a chamber against the rules. The coroner, however, was a paid employee of the mine company, Colorado Coal and Iron, and he selected three close friends of the mine supervisor as jurors. The hearings were cut short and certain testimony was not allowed. The townspeople called the procedure a cover-up of the company's dangerous mining practices.

The Jokerville never re-opened; a new, equally dangerous opening nearby was abandoned in 1895 after the coal vein narrowed.

Many other mines dotted the slopes around Crested Butte, perhaps the most famous being the Big Mine on the bench south of town. The third largest coal mine in Colorado and producer of the highest quality coal, the Big Mine ran fifty-eight years, closing in 1952.

Through much of the early twentieth century, the Colorado Fuel and Iron Company (renamed from Colorado Coal and Iron) virtually owned Crested Butte. It often paid the miners in script, basically a note of credit that could only be spent at the company's store, which often charged higher prices than other retailers. Mining officials were known to force workers to vote a certain way in town elections. Strikes by the miners seldom succeeded due to the number of immigrant workers hungry for work, and the callousness of the mine owners.

Still, mining was honest work and brought home a paycheck. The townspeople persevered, found humor and beauty where they could, and played as hard as they worked. The town rocked with the weekend's foot-stomping polkas; fraternal lodges and the Catholic Church diverted attention from the daily grind. Nursing each other through flu epidemics, sorrows and economic difficulties, the community grew strong, if not always harmonious.

As if life weren't tough enough, the town discovered another enemy — fire. With Crested Butte's wooden buildings, coal stores, explosives and continually freezing water lines, fire could quickly devour an entire block of town. Fifteen businesses burned to the ground in 1890 before firefighters gained control. So when fire broke out on Elk Avenue three

On the south side of Crested Butte, a CF&I coal tipple carried coal from the mines down into town. The railroad tracks ran beside the coal tipple and the coke ovens (on the left side of the photo), so coal could be loaded directly into the cars. Colorado Historical Society photo.

Threads from the past: Cattle still graze on open land untouched by development (right); a graveyard marker near Kebler Pass (top, far right) retells the fate of the old Irwin townsite and the dreams of those who came to the boom town; and the Old Rock School (lower, far right), completed in 1883, is being renovated to house a public library, computer lab and conference center.

years later and desperate firefighters found the water lines once again frozen, they blew up a furniture store to halt the blaze. Sure enough, the fire stopped. But the 150 pounds of explosives blew with a force that tore a gaping hole in the city hall and broke nearly every window in town.

As the demand for coal diminished and other, more convenient sources were found, the coal mines gradually closed. The closing of the Big Mine in 1952 and the removal of the Rio Grande railroad tracks shortly afterwards closed the door for many in Crested Butte. Families who had struggled for years to remain in Crested Butte finally had to

leave. Still, some held on. In 1952 a committee headed by Frank Starika searched for and found a mining company, American Smelting and Refining, to invest in the old Keystone Mine on Mt. Emmons west of Crested Butte. The Keystone erratically turned out lead, zinc, copper and silver and pumped some money back into Crested Butte, but the town dwindled to a near-ghost town of 200 residents.

The era of mining was over, but the people who had forged Crested Butte, both those who remained and those who were forced to leave, had given the town a legacy too strong to be erased. Vandenbusche concluded, "In the final analysis, it was the people who made Crested Butte what it is today. Hardened and disciplined by generations of adversity before they came to the Elk Mountains, these people took from the mountains not only coal and timber, but also bravery and tenacity, the cornerstones of any civilization."

As the local mines breathed their last, a new era began in which snow, the townspeople's long-time nemesis, became the new bounty. Hubert Smith, a doctor and attorney, sowed the seeds of tourism in 1958 with his Law/Science Academy in Crested Butte. Doctors and lawyers came to the town each summer, and its reputation as a pristine mountain hideaway quietly grew.

The old Rozman house (below), which was an isolated house on a dirt road before the ski area was started, remains a notable landmark between Crested Butte and Mt. Crested Butte. Storm-darkened mountains (right) overshadow Crested Butte in this classic view of town that has welcomed visitors and homecomers for many decades.

*S*ame street,
contrasting
images: Elk
Avenue during a
1983 blizzard
and during 1989
Fourth of July
festivities.

New faces and philosophies puzzled Crested Butte's long-time residents in the '60s and '70s. Some photos of the times: Jim Starr (above left), who is still an attorney in Crested Butte but with shorter hair and no bandana; and Bill Holland and Jude Ruddy (above right).

Although summer's pulse quickened, winter remained quiet until 1960, when Fred Rice and Dick Eflin bought the old Malensek ranch and started a ski area on Mt. Crested Butte. As though to pay its dues, the ski area struggled and finally hit bankruptcy in 1965-66. During its recovery, the ski area president, Gus Larkin, and his assistant, Nadine Israel, took turns cleaning bathrooms. The company's only phone was a pay phone: "We kept a jar of dimes on the desk to make phone calls," Israel said. Ski slopes were groomed with old box springs attached to a bicycle tire dragged down the mountainside.

The ski area also attracted waves of young people, often long-haired and full of reckless, youthful energy. Some of Crested Butte's long-time residents found the town's new role and strangely-dressed young people puzzling and threatening. Throughout the '60s, the town struggled like an adolescent caught between identities. But tourism took hold, the

young people either moved on or put down roots, and Crested Butte built on its newfound economic base.

When Howard "Bo" Callaway bought the ski area in 1970, the new Crested Butte Mountain Resort quickly expanded both ski terrain and marketing efforts. Today, Crested Butte has one of the ten largest and fastest growing ski areas in Colorado. A dozen lifts provide 800-plus acres of skiing, varying from mellow beginner slopes to the untamed Extreme Limits.

Mt. Crested Butte, incorporated in 1974 as a separate municipality three miles north of Crested Butte, provides all the modern amenities of a top-notch mountain resort — shopping centers, conference facilities, lodging for 6,000 guests ranging from budget to luxurious, restaurants and recreation facilities. Vacationers now have the plush Grande Butte Hotel, the highly-acclaimed Skyland Resort with its Robert Trent Jones II

When Amax in the late '70s proposed a huge molybdenum mine on Mt. Emmons, the High Country Citizens Alliance formed to "save the Red Lady." Above, Tracey Wickland, Marilyn Leftwich, Vinnie Rossignol, Roy Smith and other HCCA members protest the proposal at the top of Mt. Emmons. Mayor W Mitchell helped the town draw national attention for its fight against the mine.

championship golf course, and a cornucopia of other amenities.

Crested Butte's core downtown area remains somewhat like it was in the early days. Strict building codes keep the National Historic District intact, but lively colors, interesting shops and eateries, and strolling sight-seers give it new life. Around the core, Crested Butte has filled out with new homes; many of the old shacks have been remodeled.

In the late 1970s, Crested Butte made a definitive statement when it opposed a plan by Amax, Inc. to put a massive molybdenum mine on Mt. Emmons, which overlooks the town to the west. Vocal opponents (led by

166

A*nother world, three miles up the road: Where cattle grazed on open fields thirty years ago, a modern ski resort houses and entertains up to 6,000 guests. Christmas lights (left) illuminate the crane being used to build the Grande Butte Hotel in 1984; skiers (above) look down on Mt. Crested Butte and the surrounding mountains; houses now dot the flanks of Crested Butte Mountain, shown in the aerial view at right.*

the High Country Citizens Alliance and Crested Butte's mayor, W Mitchell) felt the social and environmental effects were too high a price tag for the economic boost the mine promoters promised. Legal battles between Amax and the Town of Crested Butte over watershed rights caused the plan to be indefinitely postponed. Tourism had clearly supplanted mining as the economy of choice for most of the townspeople.

Crested Butte's people may envy the pocketbooks of those in more affluent resorts; many locals still juggle several jobs during peak seasons to see them through the lean periods of the year. But Crested Butte has a

Even the movers and shakers in Crested Butte take time out for skiing. Above, Crested Butte State Bank president (and former mayor) Thom Cox; town manager (and former mayor) Bill Crank; and Ruth and Eric Roemer, owners of Penelope's, the Powerhouse, the Wooden Nickel, and other property around Crested Butte.

secure, if not rich, economy. Escorting Crested Butte into the twenty-first century has become a question of balance, not survival. The community must continue to forge a viable economy and claim a niche in a competitive and unforgiving ski industry, while preserving Crested Butte's unspoiled setting and small-town quality of life. The people must share their rare mountain home with openness, but not with greed lest they forget to protect it.

For this place comes to them as a gift — from nature, which carved a gentle valley in the midst of splendid mountains, and from men and women who defied the odds and built a town at the edge of paradise on a foundation of tenacity and love.

Lyle McNeill greets Justina Niccoli at the Two Buttes Senior Center, where the town's older residents gather for potlucks and parties. For years, Lyle has been the caretaker and host at the senior center, with its grand Masonic Hall upstairs.

Bright against the blue sky, Dean Kooiman (above) experiments with flying. His launching pad: A cliff on the North Face. Two Skyland golfers (right) go for quiet relaxation instead of adrenaline rushes.

CONTINENTAL AIRLINES

One key to Crested Butte's recent surge in popularity among skiers has been its accessibility by air. And a key to that accessibility has been Continental Airlines.

As the Official Airline of Colorado, Continental Airlines serves more Colorado cities, including Crested Butte, than any other airline.

Continental is committed to serving the needs of the traveler as never before. Expanded service to important destinations, an upgraded image including modernized interiors, attractive fares and a host of programs tailored to the needs of passengers are all part of Continental's determination to be the airline of choice for flyers everywhere.

With Continental's evolution into a truly global airline, top priority has been to add convenient departures in major business centers. A recent example is the airline's dramatic New York expansion with over 300 daily departures from the metropolitan area, making Continental the number one airline in the world's number one business market.

On international routes, Continental offers in-flight service in first and business class that is truly world class. The travel experience is enhanced by concierge service, separate check-in, priority baggage handling, full-size reclining seats, gourmet cuisine and wines voted the best of any airline in the world.

Continental also offers the award-winning OnePass℠ program and OnePass Elite, which reward customers with complimentary upgrades, bonus miles, priority boarding and expedited baggage handling.

Continental's service extends to its Presidents Clubs, private membership lounges in key airport locations which offer free local telephone calls, desks, telefax machines, photocopiers, and private conference rooms in some locations.

But Continental is making the kinds of differences that go far deeper than the fresh coat of paint adorning its planes.

The airline has put nearly all of its 25,000 customer contact people through its Quality Service Institute to offer the highest standards of service in the world. Because above all, it's the people, working around the clock, going that extra mile to make every aspect of flying more pleasureable, that make a difference.

Continental invites you to experience it on any of the airline's over 2,000 daily flights to the more than 195 destinations it reaches world-wide.

PROFILE

*Cabin,
mountain,
wreathe and bike
form a classic
Crested Butte
Christmas scene.*

ACKNOWLEDGEMENTS

Three names appear on the title page of this book, but many people actually made it possible. We would like to thank a few people personally:

For technical help:

Bruce Bartelson, geology professor at Western State College

Rosemary Smith, research coordinator, Rocky Mountain Biological Laboratory

Duane Vandenbusche, historian and professor at Western State College

Seth Adams, biology professor at Western State College

U.S. Forest Service's Gunnison personnel

Bob Gillen, vice president for corporate communication, Crested Butte Mountain Resort

Tony Fortunato, graphic artist

Martha Neumann and Katie Hagarman, Crested Butte Printing

Former Director Nadine Israel and the current staff members of the Crested Butte/Mt. Crested Butte Chamber of Commerce

The folks at the Gunnison, Western State, and Crested Butte libraries

The Colorado Historical Society in Denver

Our personal thanks:

From Sandy: To Jean and Jim Fails; Michael Garren, partner and graphics consultant incognito; Ian Hatchett, Aussie baby tender; Robbie Chula, editor and counselor; Christopher Garren, the patient toddler.

From Nathan: Aaron Kain, Howard and Susan Bilow, Abe Finkle, Warren Shelton, Ted Staidle, Joel Schulman, Phil Weinstein, Ed Andrieski, John P. Kelly, and past and present clients and models.

From all of us: To those businesses that purchased profiles and made this third printing feasible — Western State College, Continental Airlines, Crested Butte Mountain Resort and Nathan Bilow. To those who supported this project along the way, and to all who have nurtured Crested Butte through the decades.

Resource publications:

Crested Butte Primer and Part of a Winter by George Sibley

Geology of the Gunnison Country by Thomas Prather

The Gunnison Country by Duane Vandenbusche

Your Passport to the Gunnison Country by Charles Page

"History of the Rocky Mountain Biological Laboratory" by Dr. John C. Johnson, plus other RMBL resource materials

"History of Crested Butte's Buildings," article by Brenda Wiard for the Crested Butte Magazine, Winter 1989-90

Bugs DuVal (above) examines a dandelion flower in a field near his home in the early summer. With nature's wonders so omnipresent, the children in Crested Butte often become precocious naturalists.

THE PEOPLE BEHIND THE BOOK

Nathan Bilow, a resident of Crested Butte since 1979, started his photographic career in Hollywood, California, while still in high school. He now photographs for Associated Press and many major ski and outdoor publications in the United States, Asia and Europe.

Nathan traveled around the world for three years before discovering Crested Butte. He still travels extensively and photographs prolifically, but always returns to Crested Butte. He commented, "I remember returning after traveling for three months and the valley was as beautiful as anything I'd seen in my travels. It may have been the views or it may have been the feeling, but it was nice to be home."

Of his reasons for creating this book, Nathan said, "I'd like to praise the elders for preserving the land and the town, and pray that the people of the present keep it the same way so our children's children can enjoy what we enjoyed."

Sandy Fails has written about Crested Butte as reporter and editor of the *Crested Butte Chronicle and Pilot,* editor of the *Crested Butte Magazine* and national-level freelance writer.

Sandy and her husband, Michael Garren, moved to Crested Butte from Austin, Texas, in 1981 and are now raising their son, Christopher, in the mountain community. For Sandy, **Crested Butte: The Edge of Paradise** provided the chance to put into words the qualities she has grown to value in Crested Butte.

"Writing the text for this book reminded me how Crested Butte touches and changes people — through the beauty, the community, the removal from urban preoccupations. Maybe the book can rekindle for people the special sense of this place."

Jeffery Neumann has been in the printing field for twenty-one years and has operated Crested Butte Printing since 1977. Besides spending time on the press and with his wife, Martha, and children, Sarah and Tyler, Jeff serves as fire chief for the Crested Butte Fire Protection District and hunts, skis and hikes in the mountains around Crested Butte. His penchant for the outdoors he calls "a holdover from my younger days roaming the hills outside Ft. Collins."

Jeff entered the printing world at Printed in Aspen in the late 1960s. He was quickly caught up by the graphic ideas and demand for precision and quality. He brought his skills to Crested Butte in the mid-70s.

"This book, **Crested Butte: The Edge of Paradise,** began as a dream and soon became a necessary thing to produce," Jeff said. "Giving Crested Butte residents and visitors the highest quality workmanship goes with the project."